Mam

Under

Written by Ann-Marie Parker

Contents

PEARSON

What Are Marine Mammals?

Marine mammals are like land mammals except they make their home and find their food in or near the sea.

To survive in the sea, marine mammals must hold their breath under water, keep warm in icy, cold waters, and care for their young in or near their watery homes.

Dugong

Manatees and dugongs are also called sea cows. They are gentle creatures that only eat sea vegetables. A manatee has a paddle-like tail. A dugong's tail looks more like a whale's.

How Do Marine Mammals Survive Under Water?

How Marine Mammals Breathe

All marine mammals have to breathe oxygen from the air, just like humans. They are not like fish, which get their oxygen from the water through their gills or skin. Marine mammals hold their breath under water. Some whales can stay under water for as long as two hours.

- All whales breathe through a blowhole, which is a watertight valve that closes when the whale is under water.
- Whales store a lot of oxygen in their body. The oxygen is then circulated around their bodies by haemoglobin. Haemoglobin is a chemical that is found in large amounts in the body of the whale.
- A whale can exhale 90 per cent of the air in its lungs. A human can only exhale 10 per cent.
- Whales can slow down their heart rate so oxygen is only sent to the most important parts of the body, such as the heart, lungs and brain.

A whale's blowhole acts like a nostril. It breathes through the blowhole at the top of its head.

An elephant seal can hold its breath under water for one hour.

How long can some mammals hold their breath?				
Sea otters	**Humans**	**Manatees, sea lions and seals**	**Elephant seal**	**Sperm whale**
30 seconds	Couple of minutes	20 mins	One hour	Two hours

How Marine Mammals Keep Warm

Marine mammals need to spend long periods of time in the water while they are searching for food, looking after their young, migrating or resting. To be able to do this, they must have ways of insulating themselves against the cold. There are two main ways that marine mammals can do this.

Blubber:

Many marine mammals keep warm by having a thick layer of blubber or fat under their skin. This insulates the body and keeps the animal from getting cold. Blubber is also used as a source of energy during times when there is not much food available.

The layer of blubber on a whale can be up to 50 centimetres thick.

The layer of blubber on a walrus can be up to 15 centimetres thick. The blubber also protects it during fights with other walruses.

Fur:

To keep warm, sea otters have the thickest and densest fur of any mammal. If you took a microscope and looked at just one square centimetre, you would be able to count 150,000 hairs! The fur is made up of long, waterproof guard hairs and under-fur. The guard hairs keep the water from getting to the under-fur and the skin.

How Marine Mammals Care for Babies

Some marine mammals, such as whales and dolphins, give birth to their babies in water. Baby whales are called calves. They are born tail first and with their eyes open. As soon as they are born, they will swim to the surface to take their first breath.

Young blue whales drink very rich and nutritious milk from their mothers. This milk is so rich that baby blue whales can double their birth size in only seven days. Baby blue whales need to grow very quickly so that they can survive in the ocean.

Blue whale mother and baby

Dolphin mother and baby

Sea otters give birth to their young in the water, too. Their babies are called pups. The pups are born with teeth and fluffy fur that helps them float in the water. Newborn sea otters cannot swim until they are ten weeks old so they spend a lot of time lying on their mother's abdomen or floating in kelp.

Most seals and sea lions do not give birth to their babies in water. They go onto land to give birth. Harp seals have their babies on floating pieces of pack ice.

Manatees rear out of the water to allow their young to breathe and feed. The young drink milk from a nipple under the mother's armpit.

A baby harp seal drinking milk from its mother

A sea otter pup lying on its mother's abdomen

How Marine Mammals Feed

When sea otters are eating, they float on their back on the surface of the water. They use their abdomen like a table. Most sea otters eat sea creatures that they can find on the seabed, such as crabs, oysters, sea urchins and clams. When a sea otter dives for food, it will collect a rock and store it under its armpit so its front claws are free to hold its prey. Once it has surfaced, the sea otter lies on its back and smashes the shell with the rock to get at the food.

Manatees and dugongs are plant eaters. They search for plants to eat in the shallow water of rivers or streams. They produce a lot of gas in their gut from their diet of plants but this gas helps them to float in the water.

Some kinds of whales do not have teeth. Instead they have a baleen (large, horny plate), which works like a sieve. The baleen allows water to go through but traps and catches tiny sea creatures called krill. The whale can then lick the krill off with its enormous tongue. A blue whale has a tongue that is as big as an elephant.

A sea otter eating fish

A grey whale uses baleen to trap krill.

A manatee eating grasses from the sea floor

How Marine Mammals Sleep

Whales and dolphins do not fully go to sleep. Research has shown that one half of their brain always remains alert and awake while the other side sleeps. This allows the dolphin or whale to come to the surface of the water to breathe and to keep a look out for danger. If whales and dolphins were to have a deep sleep like humans do, they would drown.

Humans are 'involuntary breathers', which means that they can breathe without thinking about it, even when they are in a deep sleep. However, whales and dolphins are 'voluntary breathers', which means that they have to be alert to breathe.

Seals and sea lions do not sleep in the water. They return to land to sleep.

Sperm whales sleep upright in the water.

Seals sleep on land. They keep close for warmth and safety.

Tired sea otters sometimes wrap themselves in kelp before they go to sleep. The kelp works like an anchor on a boat, keeping the sea otter from moving too far away.

A walrus has an unusual way of sleeping in water. A walrus has pouches on either side of its head. These pouches inflate full of air and allow the walrus to rest or sleep in the water without their head slipping under the water.

A mother sea otter and her pup sleeping in kelp

Glossary

abdomen – the belly in mammals
oxygen – the life-supporting component of air

Index

Informational Explanations

Informational Explanations explain why something is the way it is or how something happens or works.

How to Write an Informational Explanation

Step One

- Select a topic.
- Write down the things you know about the topic.
- Brainstorm the questions you need to ask.

Mammals Under Water

- How do mammals survive under water?
- How do they breathe under water?
- How do they keep warm?
- How are they born?
- How do they feed under water?

Step Two

- Locate the information you need.
- Use different kinds of resources for your investigation:

Internet

Television Documentaries

Libraries

Experts...

Take notes or make copies of what you find.

Step Three

- Sort through your notes.
- Organise your information using headings.

How Marine Mammals Care for Babies
- Some mammals give birth to live young
- Babies spend a lot of time with their mothers
- Babies drink a lot of milk

How Marine Mammals Feed
- Manatees are plant eaters
- Otters use a stone to break open shells
- Some whales catch krill using their baleen

Step Four

- Use your notes to write your Explanation.
- Include an **introduction** with an opening statement:

Marine mammals are like land animals except they make their home and find their food in or near the sea…

- Include **visuals** such as…

Labels

Captions

Comparison Charts

Photographs

Your explanation could have…

a Contents page

Contents

an Index

Index

a Glossary

Glossary

abdomen – the belly in mammals

oxygen – the life-supporting component of air

Guide Notes

Title: Mammals Under Water
Stage: Advanced Fluency
Text Form: Informational Explanation
Approach: Guided Reading
Processes: Thinking Critically, Exploring Language, Processing Information
Written and Visual Focus: Captions, Labels, Index, Photographs, Comparison Chart, Glossary, Contents Page

THINKING CRITICALLY

(sample questions)

Before Reading – Establishing Prior Knowledge

- What do you know about mammals?
- What do you know about marine mammals?

Visualising the Text Content

- What might you expect to see in this book?
- What form of writing do you think will be used by the author?
- Look at the Contents page and Index. Encourage the students to think about the information and make predictions about the text content.

After Reading – Interpreting the Text

- What do you think is the purpose of this book?
- How does the introduction text on page 2 explain the idea behind the topic?
- How do you think you could find out more about the way some marine mammals gather and eat their food? What questions would you generate for the basis of your research?
- What do you think are the most important things for marine mammals to survive?
- What opinions do you have about how marine mammals compare to humans?
- What questions do you have after reading the text?
- Do you think the author explained how marine mammals can live under water? Why or Why not? What helped you understand the information?

EXPLORING LANGUAGE

Terminology

Photograph credits, diagram, index, ISBN number, contents page, glossary, comparison chart